By May Nakamura
Illustrated by Natalie Kwee

Ready-to-Read

SIMON SPOTLIGHT

An imprint of Simon & Schuster Children's Publishing Division
1230 Avenue of the Americas, New York, New York 10020
This Simon Spotlight edition September 2019
Text copyright © 2019 by Simon & Schuster, Inc.
Illustrations copyright © 2019 by Natalie Kwee
All rights reserved, including the right of reproduction in whole or in part in any form.
SIMON SPOTLIGHT, READY-TO-READ, and colophon are registered trademarks
of Simon & Schuster, Inc. For information about special discounts for bulk purchases,
please contact Simon & Schuster Special Sales at 1-866-506-1949
or business@simonandschuster.com.
Manufactured in the United States of America 0719 LAK
2 4 6 8 10 9 7 5 3 1
This book has been cataloged by the Library of Congress. LCCN 2019943694
ISBN 978-1-5344-4877-3 (hc) • ISBN 978-1-5344-4876-6 (pbk) • ISBN 978-1-5344-4878-0 (eBook)

Glossary

Accessories: fashion items that can be added to an outfit, such as hats, jewelry, gloves, scarves, belts, or purses

Costume designer: a person who designs costumes for movies, plays, or television shows

Custom-made: created just for one person

Design: a plan, sketch, or outline for a product or work of art, or the act of deciding how something will look, feel, and work

Draping: putting a fashion item on a dress form to test its design

Dress form: a life-size cloth and metal model shaped like a human's upper body that is used to help adjust the fit of patterns and garments

Fashion buyer: a person who decides what items a store will sell

Fashion designer: a person who designs clothing, shoes, or accessories like hats, gloves, purses, and more

Garment: a clothing item such as a pair of pants, a dress, or a shirt

Mood board: a collection of pictures, fabrics, trimmings, and more that is meant to help inspire or represent ideas and can be mounted onto poster board, cardboard, or other materials

Pattern: a set of shaped pieces of paper that can be used as the template, or model, for how to cut pieces of fabric, which can then be sewn together to make a garment

Ready-to-wear: clothing that is made for many different people to wear and usually made in multiple sizes so it can be bought and worn right after purchase

Sketch: to draw the main parts of something in a rough, unfinished way, or a drawing made in this style

Trend: a style that is popular

Note to readers: Some of these words may have more than one definition. The definitions above are how these words are used in this book.

Contents

Introduction

Do you like trying on clothes
and playing dress-up?
Do you love choosing
what to wear for the day?

Did you know that some people get to use their love of clothes every day as part of their jobs? When you grow up, you could work in fashion like they do!

Chapter 1:
Fashion Designer

What are you wearing today?
Everything people wear,
from sneakers to dresses,
is created by fashion designers.
To design something is to decide
how it will feel, look, and work.

Designers have to be very creative
to come up with ideas for
new garments, or clothing,
and other items like shoes.

There are many different kinds
of fashion designers.
Some work on fancy suits
while others focus on accessories
(say: ack-SESS-sore-ees)
like purses, hats, and gloves.

Some clothes are custom-made
to specifically fit the person who
buys them.
Other clothes are made in a variety
of sizes to fit different people.
These are called ready-to-wear
because you can wear them
as soon as you buy them.

Every item begins with an idea.
Some fashion designers collect
pictures, fabrics, and other things
to create a mood board.
They use this board
to help inspire ideas.

The next step is to do a sketch, which is a loose drawing of the garment. The designers also think about colors, fabrics, and details like lace and buttons.

Once a design is ready,
it is time to make the pattern.
The pattern is like a map that
shows the pieces of the garment
and how the garment will be made.
The pattern is usually made of paper.
Then the pieces are cut out
and used as a guide for how to cut
the fabric.

The fabric pieces are sewn together.
It is sort of like a jigsaw puzzle!
The garment is placed on a dress form,
which is a model of a human body
made of cloth and metal.
Designers use the dress form to
test the fit and adjust the pattern.
This is called draping.

When the design is finished
and the garment is made,
it is just the beginning.
One of the best things about being
a fashion designer is seeing your
idea come to life.
One day you might even see someone
wearing clothes you designed!

If you want to be a fashion designer, you can practice sketching ideas for clothing designs. You can also learn how to sew your own clothes!

Chapter 2:
Costume Designer

Have you ever watched a movie
and admired the outfits?
You were looking at
a costume designer's work in action!

Costume designers work
on all kinds of shows,
from television to theater.
They might design dresses for
a ballet, or a superhero outfit
for a movie!

Costumes help set the mood
and give important information
about the story.
For example, a velvet robe and crown
would tell you that an actor is a king
or a queen.

In order to make good costumes,
designers spend a lot of time
reading the show's story.
They also work closely with
directors and performers.

Costume designers sometimes research what people wore in different times and places in history. If the show is supposed to be set hundreds of years ago, a character should not be wearing a T-shirt and jeans!

If you want to be a costume designer, try to observe what people are wearing in your favorite TV show, movie, or musical.
You can also help design costumes or masks for a school play!

Chapter 3: Fashion Buyer

You don't have to be a designer
to work in fashion.
You can be a fashion buyer!
They buy items from designers.
They decide what a store should sell
to customers like you.

Buyers pay attention to trends,
or styles that are popular
in fashion and design.
If the color red is becoming popular,
they might make sure their store
has a lot of red pants!

Fashion buyers also take risks. They try to guess future trends, and sometimes they guess wrong. They also try to predict how long trends will last.

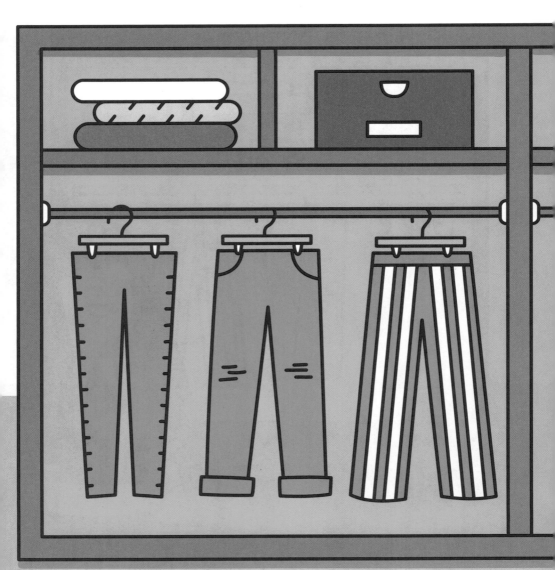

Sometimes trends change quickly, and everyone starts wearing blue pants instead of red pants!

A buyer's job combines fashion
and math. They look at past
sales numbers to decide what to buy.
The ideal clothing item looks good
and fits many people well, which will
make people more likely to buy it
and make money for the store.

Buyers must also think about
the price of items.
Shoes covered in diamonds might
sound pretty, but if they cost a lot
of money, they might not sell.

$10,000.00

Some stores have more than one
buyer. Each person focuses on
a different fashion category,
like pajamas or shoes.

If you want to be a fashion buyer,
you can practice observing what
people wear.
What styles and colors do you see?
With practice you'll become
good at noticing fashion trends!

Clothes are not just for warmth.
They can also be a way to express
who you are.

Maybe someday when you grow up, you will help create the next big fashion trend!

Fashion designer, costume designer, and fashion buyer are just a few cool jobs for people who love fashion. Turn the page to discover even more!

More Cool Fashion Jobs!

A **fashion journalist** (say: JUHR-null-list) writes articles about fashion news. They might interview people and attend fashion shows, where fashion designers present their new clothing or accessories.

A **fashion marketer** researches fashion trends and finds ways to get people to notice products so that people will buy them.

A **fashion publicist** (say: PUHB-liss-sist) provides information about a fashion brand to the public and tries to make the brand look good. They plan fashion shows, talk to fashion journalists, and more.

A **personal stylist** helps someone choose what clothes to buy and wear. They put together outfits that are specially styled just for one person!

A **patternmaker** creates the patterns for a fashion item. They make sure that the patterns' sizes and shapes all fit together to make something you can actually wear.

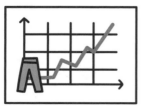

A **trend forecaster** predicts what kinds of colors and styles will be popular in the future. Sometimes they predict fashion trends more than two years ahead!